THE OFFICIAL
ANNUAL 2023

WRITTEN BY STEVE BARTRAM
DESIGNED BY DANIEL JAMES

A Grange Publication

© 2022. Published by Grange Communications Ltd, Edinburgh, under
licence from Manchester United Football Club. Printed in the EU.

Photography © MUFC

ISBN: 978-1-915295-52-1

CONTENTS

WELCOME

TO THE 2023 MANCHESTER UNITED ANNUAL!

The 2022/23 campaign marked a new chapter for the Reds under the management of Erik ten Hag, and we kick off this year's Annual by looking at the Dutch tactician's road to Old Trafford, with insight from those who have worked with him along the way.

We profile some of your favourite United players, including the newcomers who joined at the start of the season, and captain Katie Zelem runs through the United Women's squad – including those who were part of England's European Championship-winning squad!

To celebrate the Premier League's 30th anniversary, we take a statistical look at why United are the division's main draw, plus we salute the historic achievements of club legend Cristiano Ronaldo and the FA Youth Cup-winning antics of the latest batch of young Reds.

There's all of this and plenty more besides in The 2023 Manchester United Annual. Test your knowledge of the Reds with a bumper quiz section, then enter our competition to win a United shirt signed by men's squad members!

Oh, and remember to keep the Red flag flying high!

ERIK TEN HAG

"THERE'S NOTHING ON EARTH LIKE BEING A RED"

MANCHESTER UNITED MANAGER

THE TEN HAG ERA BEGINS

In the summer of 2022, United appointed Erik ten Hag as new permanent manager, and the Dutchman quickly set about putting his stamp on the club. The Reds' players certainly approve of Ten Hag's approach – here's what the lads think of Erik's impact at Old Trafford…

WORKING TOGETHER

"The manager knows 100 per cent what he wants. He knows the way he wants to play. He's giving a lot of information to the team, trying to give the details and have some rules inside and outside the pitch, I think this is what we need and also to know what we have to do on the pitch and play as a team. The whole team is working very hard. They are very intense sessions with the manager, he knows very clearly what he wants for the team and there is a lot of information. It's very intense training and everyone is focused on football and I feel that I have seen great, great things."

- DAVID DE GEA

SETTING THE STANDARD

"He knows what the team needs and he has his own style and how he wants to manage. All the players have really taken it on board and they're really enjoying it. He is very hands-on and he takes a lot of the sessions. He's involved a lot and if he sees people aren't hitting the standards that he wants in training he'll make sure they know. That's good because he keeps the standards high."

- LUKE SHAW

NEW TACTICS

"We have been much more aggressive now and the three guys up front have been much more aggressive in the way they press. They make the last line squeeze and it makes the midfielders come a little bit higher. It makes it so, when we recover the ball, we are being closer to the ball too. We are much fresher to do that, and we have freedom when we recover the ball, because we get to teams and, when they recover, they are really wide. There is loads of space in the middle and we are much better on the ball too."

- BRUNO FERNANDES

HARDER, FITTER, FASTER, STRONGER

"Whenever you've got a new manager, there's a lot of new ideas, a lot of things we have to take on board in terms of what the manager wants from us, which is important. Everyone's so, so happy with the coach in terms of the detail and attention to the work that we're doing, and everyone's so fit now. And we can get fitter, I can get fitter, the whole team can, which is obviously a benefit for the future as well."

- SCOTT McTOMINAY

TOUGH LOVE

"We need to be ready to hear things that maybe we don't want to hear – everything is for the greater good of the team and that's the most important thing. I feel that we start from scratch: new manager, new energy, new players coming in and we need to build a team, a staff, a club, everyone together and go forward. We need to be proactive – everyone. Read the game, be always on our toes. Mentally we have to be connected all the time."

- DIOGO DALOT

TEN HAG'S ROAD TO UNITED

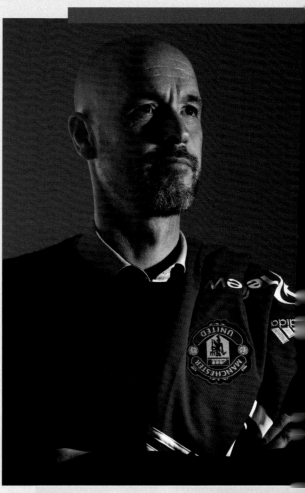

2002-09 | FC TWENTE

YOUTH COACH, THEN ASSISTANT MANAGER

"The amount of detail, the planning, how he wants his team to play, the discipline both on and off the field, the demands of the game, the style of football… I knew from day one that Erik was special and he has gone on to prove that. I've always followed his career and it's always been a learning experience and I think that's how you can sum Erik up. He's a teacher, he's a learner, he's a fanatic about the game. Engrossed with the game. He works 24/7 and he must be thinking 24/7 about football."

- STEVE McCLAREN, FORMER FC TWENTE MANAGER

2009-12 | PSV EINDHOVEN

ASSISTANT MANAGER

"He was always talking with [PSV manager] Fred Rutten and he learnt a lot, I think, from him. On the training pitch he was phenomenal, he's a real coach that practices what he's doing. They were always looking for options, and Erik and Fred always were talking about solutions. When this happens, what are we going to do then, when that happens, what will we do. Fred gave him a big opportunity when he took him to PSV as assistant coach, and I don't think any of us are surprised to see how he's gone on to be a great manager."

- SJAAK POLAK, FORMER TEAM-MATE

2012-13 | GO AHEAD EAGLES

MANAGER

"He started with his philosophy, took us with him. It was a change for a lot of players because he said: 'I work hard, the staff work hard, so if we do that then we can say to the players that they have to work hard as well. We have to do it as a team.'"

- DENNIS DEMMERS, FORMER GO AHEAD EAGLES COACH

2013-15 | BAYERN MUNICH

RESERVES MANAGER

"He was so good in details on the pitch. He had a clear philosophy on the pitch. We had very long training sessions and he wanted to be perfect in every detail. We were really impressed about everything he coached us: every passing drill, every rondo, every training session."

- TOBIAS SCHWEINSTEIGER, FORMER BAYERN MUNICH II PLAYER

2015-17 | FC UTRECHT

MANAGER

"He changed a lot in our whole way of thinking in Utrecht, changed a lot inside the whole organisation. He made it way more professional. The pitches, the food, the players had to spend way longer at the club. The whole mindset of Utrecht changed."

- RICK KRUYS, FORMER UTRECHT COACH

2017-2022 | AJAX

MANAGER

"Ajax is very particular in the coaches they give jobs. They did a great job by signing Erik. Some people were sceptical, but he proved himself to be one of the best coaches Ajax ever had. He had to make sure Ajax didn't lose the Ajax way of playing, but at the same time he wanted to put his vision on the modern game. Without the ball, he wanted to intercept it as soon as possible. With the ball, he wanted to play beautiful football. He knows what he wants as a coach, he has a clear vision and he demands the best from his players to execute how he wants to play."

- RYAN BABEL, FORMER AJAX PLAYER

THROUGHOUT THE ANNUAL WE'LL BE PROFILING A SELECTION OF REDS FROM ACROSS ERIK'S FIRST-TEAM SQUAD, KICKING OFF WITH DAVID AND RAPHAEL...

DAVID DE GEA

1

POSITION — GOALKEEPER

> **MANCHESTER IS MY HOME. I FEEL VERY GOOD HERE. IT'S A PRIVILEGE, IT'S AN HONOUR TO BE HERE IN THIS CLUB. IT'S ONE OF THE BEST THINGS IN MY LIFE, TO BE A PART OF THIS CLUB.**

DAVID ON HIS LOVE FOR UNITED

 BORN: 7 NOVEMBER 1990; MADRID, SPAIN

Nobody in United's squad has more experience at the club than David de Gea. The 2011 arrival from Atletico Madrid was just 20 when he moved for the second-highest ever fee for a goalkeeper, but that outlay has been heavily justified ever since. In his first 11 seasons as a Red, the Spaniard moved to the brink of 500 outings for the club, building a reputation as one of the world's greatest stoppers and picking up a joint-record four Sir Matt Busby Player of the Year awards.

"DAVID'S SHOWN HE'S A WORLD-CLASS GOALKEEPER, A GREAT SHOT-STOPPER. HE'S PLAYED SOME MAGNIFICENT FOOTBALL IN HIS CAREER. SINCE I'VE BEEN HERE, IT'S PROBABLY BEEN HIS BEST FORM."

HARRY MAGUIRE

DID YOU KNOW?

Going into the 2022/23 season, David needed just 16 more clean sheets to overtake Alex Stepney (175) and Peter Schmeichel (180) as the goalkeeper with the most shutouts in United's history.

RAPHAEL VARANE

POSITION ⬡ **DEFENDER**

19

🇫🇷 **BORN: 25 APRIL 1993;
LILLE, FRANCE**

When a player captains his country at the tender age of 21, he is clearly a special talent, and France's youngest-ever skipper, Raphael Varane, has long-since proven his pedigree. United first tried to sign him at 18 from Lens, but he was persuaded to join Real Madrid instead and, after he'd won 18 major honours during a decade in Spain, the Reds finally got their man in the summer of 2021. Blessed with pace, intellect and a hulking physique, Rapha is a thoroughbred defender of the highest calibre.

DID YOU KNOW?

Rapha was the only player in Didier Deschamps' squad to play every single second of France's successful 2018 World Cup campaign in Russia, starring in all seven of Les Bleus' fixtures.

" IT WAS A SPECIAL MOMENT FOR ME AND MY FAMILY. IT'S AMAZING TO MEET A PERSON LIKE HIM AT 18. YOU KNOW, AFTER THAT, IT'S YOUR DESTINY. TEN YEARS IN MADRID AND NOW I'M HERE. "

**RAPHAEL ON SIR
ALEX'S ATTEMPTS TO
SIGN HIM IN 2011**

"RAPHA IS A WINNER. EVERYONE KNOWS THAT. HE'S A NICE GUY AND WORKS REALLY HARD, AND IS ALWAYS PUSHING EVERYONE TO DO BETTER. HE HAS A GREAT MENTALITY AND HE IS REALLY IMPORTANT FOR US. HE'S A LEADER."

BRUNO FERNANDES

RONNY THE RECORD BREAKER

Cristiano Ronaldo is one of football's living legends, a leading contender for the title of GOAT and – as he showed in the first season of his second stint at United – he's very much still got it. Here's a breakdown of his unbelievable career records to date. Altogether now…SIUUUUU!

CRISTIANO RONALDO

MOST INTERNATIONAL GOALS EVER

In September 2021, Cristiano headed two late goals to not only give Portugal a dramatic 2-1 win over Republic of Ireland, he also overtook Iran's Ali Daei as the leading international goalscorer. Daei is the only other player to pass 100 goals for his country, notching 109, but Cristiano moved past him and has kept going, starting the 2022/23 season on 117.

MOST INTERNATIONAL HAT-TRICKS EVER

Amongst his 815 career goals, Cristiano has hit a jaw-dropping 60 hat-tricks, 10 of them for Portugal between 2013 and 2021. That makes him the scorer of the most trebles in the history of international football. They've all come in competitive games, too – so no stat-padding in friendlies. To boot, he's also the oldest hat-trick scorer at a World Cup, following his 2018 trio against Spain!

MOST EUROPEAN CHAMPIONSHIP GOALS

Thanks to his heroics for Portugal, Cristiano is comfortably perched atop the all-time scoring chart for the European Championship with 14. He's the only player in double figures and has scored at a record five editions of the tournament, bagging at Euro 2004, 2008, 2012, 2016 and 2020. Three of them came as Portugal won the tournament for the first time in 2016.

MOST CHAMPIONS LEAGUE GOALS

During 2021/22, United's no.7 scored in five of the Reds' six Champions League group stage games, taking his personal haul to 140 in the world's finest club competition – 15 ahead of nearest rival Lionel Messi. For good measure, Ronny also netted a Champions League qualifying goal against Debreceni in 2005, but UEFA only counts goals scored in the competition proper.

MOST CHAMPIONS LEAGUE ASSISTS

Demonstrating that he's not solely about looking to score himself, Cristiano is also the leading assists-maker in Champions League history, with a staggering 42 set-ups putting him at the top of the assist chart too. Once again, second spot goes to Lionel Messi, who had 36 going into the 2022/23 season.

MOST CHAMPIONS LEAGUE APPEARANCES

With 183 outings, Ronny is the leading appearance-maker in Champions League history, six ahead of former Real Madrid team-mate Iker Casillas, who retired in 2020. Among active players, Cristiano is far and away the leader, with Messi on 156 and Karim Benzema on 142.

MOST GOALS IN WORLD FOOTBALL EVER

Going into 2022/23, Cristiano had amassed 815 career goals, more than any other player in the history of competitive football. That breaks down as five for Sporting Lisbon, 118 in his first spell at United, 450 for Real Madrid, 101 for Juventus and another 24 for the Reds. Oh, and just another 117 goals for Portugal on top of that. Mindblowing, and he's not done scoring yet!

LISANDRO MARTINEZ

POSITION ⬠ **DEFENDER**

6

> "YOU HAVE TO TAKE RESPONSIBILITY FOR YOURSELF. YOU HAVE TO BE A MAN. THEN YOU HAVE TO FIGHT FOR EVERYTHING. YOU HAVE TO FIGHT FOR FOOD, YOU HAVE TO FIGHT FOR YOUR FAMILY, YOU HAVE TO FIGHT FOR YOUR TEAM. THEN YOU LEARN A LOT: HOW HARD LIFE IS."

MARTINEZ ON LEAVING HOME AT 14 TO FORGE A FOOTBALL CAREER

 BORN: 18 JANUARY 1998; GUALEGUAY, ARGENTINA

When Erik ten Hag took charge at Old Trafford, he quickly identified the need to sign a centre-back who could dominate opposing forwards while also contributing to United's attacks. His search took him straight back to Ajax to sign Argentina international Lisandro Martinez, who improved so much in three seasons with Ten Hag that he evolved into one of Europe's smartest defenders. Named Ajax's player of the year in 2021/22, Lisandro is also very capable in midfield and on the left side of defence, making him an extremely valuable arrival.

> "HE'S A DEFENDER THAT IS VERY EASY ON THE EYE AND HE HAS THAT AGGRESSIVE NATURE THAT YOU EXPECT FROM AN ARGENTINIAN DEFENDER – HE'S TOUGH, AND HE IS VERY CLEVER IN THE WAY THAT HE POSITIONS HIMSELF. AS A CENTRE BACK, YOU DON'T NEED TO BE BIG TO DO WELL IN ENGLAND, YOU NEED TO BE CLEVER."

FORMER UNITED AND AJAX DEFENDER JAAP STAM

DID YOU KNOW?

Lisandro's hero as a youngster was former United and Argentina star Gabriel Heinze. As a hard, left-footed Argentinian defender with a love for making tackles, it's easy to see why!

TYRELL MALACIA

POSITION ⬡ DEFENDER

12

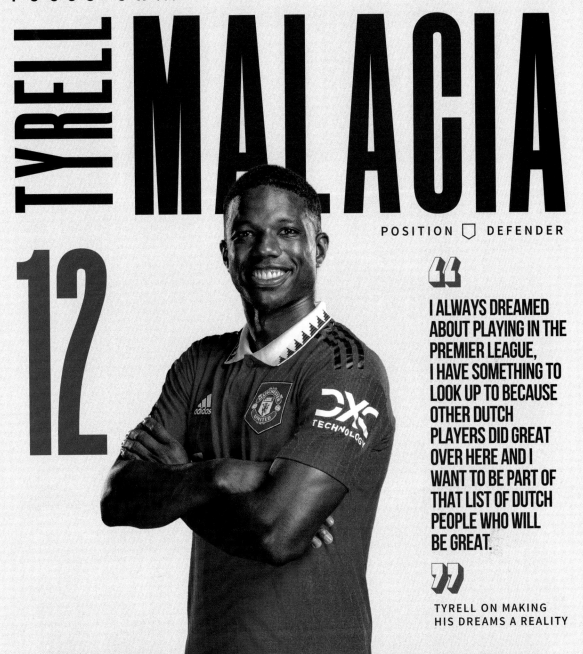

> **I ALWAYS DREAMED ABOUT PLAYING IN THE PREMIER LEAGUE, I HAVE SOMETHING TO LOOK UP TO BECAUSE OTHER DUTCH PLAYERS DID GREAT OVER HERE AND I WANT TO BE PART OF THAT LIST OF DUTCH PEOPLE WHO WILL BE GREAT.**

TYRELL ON MAKING HIS DREAMS A REALITY

"TYRELL HAS BEEN GREAT SINCE HE'S BEEN HERE. I USED TO PLAY AGAINST HIM IN THE NATIONAL TEAM AS WELL, WHEN I WAS YOUNGER, SO I'VE KNOWN ABOUT HIM FOR A LONG TIME AND I KNOW HE'S A GREAT FULL-BACK."

JADON SANCHO

With an infectious smile and a happy-go-lucky personality, Tyrell Malacia arrived at Old Trafford in the summer of 2022 and became an instantly likeable member of Erik ten Hag's squad. Put him on a football pitch, however, and the young Netherlands international is all business. A fans' favourite at his boyhood club, Feyenoord, Malacia earned himself a reputation as one of the toughest-tackling defenders in the Dutch league, and his no-nonsense approach and skilful ball work in England saw him quickly impress United supporters too.

 BORN: 17 AUGUST 1999; ROTTERDAM, NETHERLANDS

DID YOU KNOW?

Malacia's style of play is so determined that Feyenoord fans called him 'The Pitbull' – the same nickname given to aggressive Dutch legend Edgar Davids.

BACK ON TOUR

For the first time since 2019, United were able to go on pre-season tour in 2022. Taking in Thailand, Australia and Norway, the trip went down well with Reds all over the world!

MAN UTD TOUR BANGKOK 2022

THAI REDS SHOW THEIR LOVE!

BANGKOK
★ THAILAND ★
JULY 2022
RECEIVED

TONY HELPS DOWN LIVERPOOL!

NANI AND ALBERT REUNITED

JULY 2022
MELBOURNE
AUSTRALIA

TOUR 2022 TOUR 2022 TOUR 2022

THE GOALS KEEP COMING

PACKED OUT IN PERTH!

SIGNING OFF IN NORWAY

AUSTRALIA
PERTH
JULY 2022

BRUNO CAN I HAVE YOUR SHIRT

RASHFORD CAN I HAVE YOUR SHIRT

NORWAY
★ ★ ★
APPROVED
OSLO

BRUNO FERNANDES

8

POSITION — MIDFIELDER

"I GREW UP WATCHING THIS TEAM, DREAMING OF GETTING THE CHANCE TO PLAY HERE ONE DAY. THAT DREAM IS NOW A REALITY AND AN HONOUR. IT FEELS AMAZING TO STEP OUT AT OLD TRAFFORD, TO HEAR THE FANS SING MY SONG AND TO SCORE IN FRONT OF THE STRETFORD END. THERE IS SO MUCH MORE THAT I WANT TO ACHIEVE HERE."

BRUNO ON FULFILLING HIS CHILDHOOD DREAM

"HE'S BETTER THAN ME. HE'S DIFFERENT TO ME. HE SCORES MORE GOALS THAN ME, HE CREATES MORE GOALS THAN ME. I'D LIKE TO PLAY WITH HIM."

REDS LEGEND PAUL SCHOLES

BORN: 8 SEPTEMBER 1994; MAIA, PORTUGAL

Few signings have made as much impact on United's fortunes as Bruno Fernandes. The Portuguese playmaker arrived midway through the 2019/20 campaign while the Reds were struggling, and he immediately transformed the team's approach. A regular scorer and maker of goals, Bruno instantly became a fans' favourite with his all-action approach and vocal leadership of the team. After signing a new, long-term contract in 2022 and switching to his preferred no.8 shirt, the future looks bright for United's Portuguese magnifico.

DID YOU KNOW?

The no.8 shirt holds special meaning for Bruno, whose dad used to wear that shirt during his playing career, so he was thrilled to inherit it from Juan Mata. "I was always joking with Juan and saying that he has to change clubs so I can use my number again," he said. "We joked a lot about that!"

CHRISTIAN ERIKSEN

> **IT'S A CLUB WITH A LOT OF HISTORY. A LOT OF BIG, BIG PLAYERS HAVE BEEN HERE, AND I'M HERE TO PLAY AND PROVE THAT I CAN BE ON THAT LIST. IT'S A BIG LIST WITH SOME VERY, VERY BIG NAMES.**

ERIKSEN ON UNITED'S HISTORY OF GIFTED PLAYMAKERS

14

POSITION — MIDFIELDER

BORN: 14 FEBRUARY 1992; MIDDELFART, DENMARK

Frequently during his seven years at Tottenham, Christian Eriksen was a thorn in United's side. The Danish playmaker would repeatedly find space and cause havoc, making him a nightmare to defend against. His shock short-term move to Brentford in 2022 brought him back to English football from Internazionale, and United pounced at the opportunity to recruit the brilliant Denmark international on a free transfer ahead of the 2022/23 campaign. Whether in attacking midfield or a slightly withdrawn role, Christian is the man to join the dots in United's forward play.

DID YOU KNOW?

Christian has been on United's radar for a long time. Media reports began linking the Reds with a move for him when the midfielder was just 18, 12 years before the deal finally happened!

> **"HE'S AN ATTACKING TYPE OF PLAYER, BUT HE'S DISCIPLINED, AND HE DOES WORK HARD FOR THE TEAM, AND HE GETS BACK INTO THE RIGHT AREAS. HE'S GOT AMAZING QUALITY ON THE BALL."**

MIDFIELD LEGEND BRYAN ROBSON

UNITED AND THE WORLD CUP

In celebration of the 2022 World Cup, here's a brief history of United's involvement in international football's biggest tournament...

FORWARD

SIR BOBBY CHARLTON
ENGLAND, 1966

MIDFIELDER

NOBBY STILES
ENGLAND, 1966

FORWARD

JOHN CONNELLY
ENGLAND, 1966

GOALKEEPER

FABIEN BARTHEZ
FRANCE, 1998

DEFENDER

LAURENT BLANC
FRANCE, 1998

MIDFIELDER

KLEBERSON
BRAZIL, 2002

GERARD PIQUE
SPAIN, 2010

JUAN MATA
SPAIN, 2010

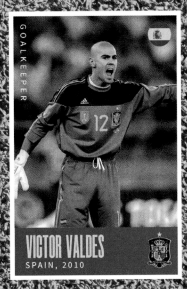

VICTOR VALDES
SPAIN, 2010

BASTIAN SCHWEINSTEIGER
GERMANY, 2014

PAUL POGBA
FRANCE, 2018

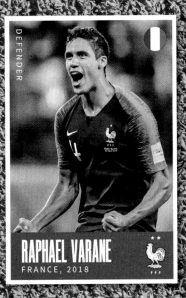

RAPHAEL VARANE
FRANCE, 2018

UNITED'S WORLD CUP WINNERS

United have had 12 first-team players who lifted the World Cup trophy at some stage in their career, and only four of them have won it while on United's books. That quartet is made up of Bobby Charlton, John Connelly and Nobby Stiles, who all starred in England's 1966 win, plus Paul Pogba, who made his own piece of history by becoming the only United player to score in a World Cup final during France's 2018 win over Croatia. Alongside the midfielder was Raphael Varane, who is now the only World Cup winner in United's current squad.

Gold Shiny = Was a United player when they won the trophy

AN ALL-TIME SHOCKER

United's John Aston Senior was part of a World Cup game which became so famous, it was the subject of both a book and a movie! The defender was part of the England side strongly expected to hammer USA in Brazil, but the unfancied Americans – who were semi-professional players – stunned the tournament favourites with a 1-0 win in Belo Horizonte. The Americans were so unexpectedly impressive that Matt Busby subsequently signed temporary captain Ed McIlvenney for United. The result remains one of the all-time great World Cup upsets, so much so that in 1996, a book about the encounter entitled The Game of Their Lives was released, and it was made into a movie in 2005.

DEFENDER

JOHN ASTON SENIOR
ENGLAND

GOALKEEPER

HARRY GREGG
NORTHERN IRELAND

HARRY'S INCREDIBLE COMEBACK

Reds goalkeeper Harry Gregg was renowned as one of the heroes of the Munich Air Disaster, in which he returned to the plane's wreckage to save his team-mates. Despite going through such a horrifying experience in February 1958, Harry returned to action almost immediately and was named in Northern Ireland's World Cup squad just four months later. If that wasn't incredible enough, he performed so well at the tournament in Sweden that he was named in the All-Star Team of the World Cup!

NO PLACE LIKE HOME

Old Trafford has its own World Cup links, having been one of the stadia chosen to stage games when England were tournament hosts in 1966. Three group stage matches took place at the Theatre of Dreams: Portugal 3-1 Hungary, Portugal 3-0 Bulgaria and Hungary 3-1 Bulgaria.

OLD TRAFFORD
MANCHESTER, 1966

MIDFIELDER

BRYAN ROBSON
ENGLAND VS FRANCE, 1982

RECORD-BREAKING ROBBO

Reds legend Bryan Robson has a special place in tournament history, having scored the fastest goal in the World Cup – ever! The all-action midfielder required just 27 seconds to open the scoring for England against France at the 1982 edition in Spain. He also scored a second goal later in the game to help secure a 3-1 win for the Three Lions.

BIG NORM SETS THE STANDARD

After making just two appearances for United at the end of the 1981/82 season, teenage forward Norman Whiteside was hurried into Northern Ireland's squad for the 1982 World Cup in Spain. He made his international debut in the opening group stage game against Yugoslavia aged just 17 years and 41 days, making him the youngest player in tournament history, beating the previous record set by Brazilian legend Pele!

FORWARD

NORMAN WHITESIDE
NORTHERN IRELAND

BECKS, BECKS, BECKS

England star David Beckham is the only United player to score in three editions of the World Cup, bagging goals for the Three Lions in 1998, 2002 and 2006. Bobby Charlton, Marouane Fellaini, Ji-sung Park and Javier Hernandez all managed to score in two separate tournaments.

DAVID BECKHAM
ENGLAND, 2006

DAVID BECKHAM
ENGLAND, 2002

DAVID BECKHAM
ENGLAND, 2006

JAVIER HERNANDEZ
MEXICO, 2014

SIX SIMULTANEOUS REDS

At the 2014 World Cup in Brazil, a remarkable six United players scored at least once for their respective countries. Robin van Persie (managed by incoming Reds boss Louis van Gaal for Holland), Marouane Fellaini, Nani, Wayne Rooney, Javier Hernandez and Juan Mata all found the net during the group stage, while Marcos Rojo scored for Argentina before joining United two months later.

ROBIN AND ROMELU TIED

The most goals scored by a United player at a single World Cup is four, an honour shared by Robin van Persie and Romelu Lukaku at the 2014 and 2018 tournaments respectively. England's Bobby Charlton scored three times at the 1966 tournament, as did Jesper Olsen for Denmark in 1986.

ROMELU LUKAKU
BELGIUM, 2018

ROBIN VAN PERSIE
NETHERLANDS, 2018

SIR BOBBY CHARLTON
ENGLAND, 1966

GOALS, GOALS, GOALS

In total, 22 players have scored for their countries at World Cups while on United's books. The very first was Sir Bobby Charlton, who netted for England against Argentina in Chile back in 1962, while the most recent prior to the 2022 tournament was Paul Pogba, who bagged for France in their 2018 final win over Croatia.

PAUL POGBA
FRANCE, 2018

Here's the full list of each scorer and their country, in chronological order:

Bobby Charlton (England), Joe Jordan (Scotland), Jesper Olsen (Denmark), Norman Whiteside (Northern Ireland), Gordon Strachan (Scotland), Paul Scholes (England), David Beckham (England), Quinton Fortune (South Africa), Diego Forlan (Uruguay), Cristiano Ronaldo (Portugal), Ruud van Nistelrooy (Netherlands), Ji-sung Park (South Korea), Javier Hernandez (Mexico), Robin van Persie (Netherlands), Marouane Fellaini (Belgium), Wayne Rooney (England), Nani (Portugal), Juan Mata (Spain), Romelu Lukaku (Belgium), Marcos Rojo (Argentina), Jesse Lingard (England), Paul Pogba (France).

DIEGO FORLAN
URUGUAY, 2002

CRISTIANO RONALDO
PORTUGAL, 2006

POSITION ⟶ MIDFIELDER

CASEMIRO

18

> I'M ENDING ONE BEAUTIFUL JOURNEY IN MADRID WHILST STARTING ANOTHER IN MANCHESTER AS DETERMINED AS EVER TO WIN FOOTBALL MATCHES, WIN TROPHIES AND MAKE OUR FANS PROUD BY BRINGING SUCCESS TO THIS GREAT CLUB.

CASEMIRO ON FACING A NEW CHALLENGE IN ENGLAND

 BORN: 23 FEBRUARY 1992; SAO JOSE DOS CAMPOS, BRAZIL

When Erik ten Hag sought to bring balance to his midfield at Old Trafford, he quickly concluded that Casemiro was an ideal transfer target. The Brazilian international joined the Reds late in the 2022 summer transfer window to huge fanfare and excitement among team-mates, staff and supporters, all of whom were thrilled by the arrival of one of the modern game's finest defensive midfielders. A serial trophy-winner with Real Madrid and Brazil, Casemiro arrived with one of the finest pedigrees in world football and – more importantly – the desire to keep improving it at Old Trafford.

"FIRST AND FOREMOST, HE'S A TOP PLAYER. I'M HAPPY TO BE ABLE TO PLAY ALONGSIDE HIM BOTH HERE AT MANCHESTER UNITED AND IN THE BRAZILIAN NATIONAL TEAM. HE'S A TOP GUY AND HIS TRACK RECORD SPEAKS FOR ITSELF. HE'S HAD A GLITTERING CAREER AND PLAYED FOR REAL MADRID FOR MANY YEARS. IT'S AN HONOUR TO HAVE HIM AS A TEAM-MATE."

FRED

DID YOU KNOW?

Casemiro has four Champions League winners' medals (he missed the 2014 final, otherwise he'd have had five), putting him joint-second in the competition's all-time rankings. Only Karim Benzema, Dani Carvajal, Luka Modric and Cristiano Ronaldo have more, with five each.

POSITION ☐ FORWARD

ANTONY

> **REAL PRESSURE WAS WHEN I LIVED IN A FAVELA AND LEFT FOR SCHOOL AT NINE IN THE MORNING, NOT SURE WHETHER I WOULD BE ABLE TO EAT AGAIN UNTIL NINE AT NIGHT. THAT'S SOME PRESSURE. OTHERWISE, WE CAN ALL ADAPT.**

ANTONY ON COPING WITH EXPECTATION IN FOOTBALL

BORN: 24 FEBRUARY 2000; OSASCO, BRAZIL

DID YOU KNOW?

Antony was part of the Brazil squad which triumphed at the 2020 Olympics, making him just the sixth gold medallist to represent United. Five of the others are Argentinian – Angel Di Maria, Gabriel Heinze, Sergio Romero and Carlos Tevez – and the very first was Reds forward (and future chairman), Harold Hardman, who was part of Team GB's success at the 1908 games in London.

Born and raised in a tough part of Brazil's Sao Paulo, fleet-footed forward Antony blends street smarts and silky skills in the United attack. After joining Ajax in 2020, the youngster enjoyed two sensational years in Holland, scoring or assisting 47 times, before convincing United to make him a key part of Erik ten Hag's squad. Blessed with pace to burn and tonnes of trickery, the Brazilian international forward is one of the most exciting additions to arrive at Old Trafford in years.

> "IT MAY SEEM LIKE HE'S JUST A BOY, THAT THINGS ARE MOVING TOO FAST FOR HIM AND HE DOESN'T HAVE MUCH EXPERIENCE. BUT EVERY COACH THAT WORKS WITH HIM DOESN'T WANT TO LET HIM GO. THEY HAVE A DIFFERENT PERCEPTION OF ANTONY BECAUSE THEY KNOW THE PHENOMENON THAT HE IS IN THE DAILY WORK, THE ABSURD THINGS THAT HE DOES WITH THE BALL, HOW TALENTED HE IS."

ALEXANDRE PASSARO, FORMER SAO PAULO DIRECTOR

BOSSES OF THE PREMIER LEAGUE ERA

As the Premier League celebrates its 30th anniversary in 2022/23, look at the starring role played by United's players during the top-flight over the last three decades...*

13 PREMIER LEAGUE TITLES

1. **MANCHESTER UNITED – 13**
2. MANCHESTER CITY – 6
3. CHELSEA – 5
4. ARSENAL – 3
5. BLACKBURN ROVERS – 1
6. LEICESTER CITY – 1
7. LIVERPOOL – 1

1. **MANCHESTER UNITED | 703**
2. ARSENAL | 619
3. CHELSEA | 618
4. LIVERPOOL | 609
5. TOTTENHAM HOTSPUR | 502
6. MANCHESTER CITY | 473
7. EVERTON | 418
8. NEWCASTLE UNITED | 382
9. ASTON VILLA | 354
10. WEST HAM UNITED | 335

703 WINS

2,185 GOALS

1. MANCHESTER UNITED | 2,185
2. LIVERPOOL | 2,021
3. ARSENAL | 2,017
4. CHELSEA | 1,973
5. TOTTENHAM HOTSPUR | 1,745
6. MANCHESTER CITY | 1,658
7. EVERTON | 1,491
8. NEWCASTLE UNITED | 1,377
9. ASTON VILLA | 1,265
10. WEST HAM UNITED | 1,235

478 CLEAN SHEETS

1. MANCHESTER UNITED | 478
2. CHELSEA | 463
3. LIVERPOOL | 442
4. ARSENAL | 436
5. EVERTON | 350
6. MANCHESTER CITY | 334
7. TOTTENHAM HOTSPUR | 330
8. ASTON VILLA | 301
9. NEWCASTLE UNITED | 267
10. WEST HAM UNITED | 259

INDIVIDUAL STATISTICS

APPEARANCES

1. GARETH BARRY | 653
2. RYAN GIGGS | 632
3. FRANK LAMPARD | 609
4. JAMES MILNER | 588
5. DAVID JAMES | 572
6. GARY SPEED | 535
7. EMILE HESKEY | 516
8. MARK SCHWARZER | 514
9. JAMIE CARRAGHER | 508
10. PHIL NEVILLE | 505

GOALS

1. ALAN SHEARER | 260
2. WAYNE ROONEY | 208
3. ANDY COLE | 187
4. SERGIO AGÜERO | 184
5. HARRY KANE | 183
6. FRANK LAMPARD | 177
7. THIERRY HENRY | 175
8. ROBBIE FOWLER | 163
9. JERMAIN DEFOE | 162
10. MICHAEL OWEN | 150

ASSISTS

1. RYAN GIGGS | 162
2. CESC FÀBREGAS | 111
3. WAYNE ROONEY | 103
4. FRANK LAMPARD | 102
5. DENNIS BERGKAMP | 94
6. DAVID SILVA | 93
7. STEVEN GERRARD | 92
=8. KEVIN DE BRUYNE | 86
=8. JAMES MILNER | 86
10. DAVID BECKHAM | 80

1. PETR CECH | 202
2. DAVID JAMES | 169
3. MARK SCHWARZER | 151
4. DAVID SEAMAN | 141
5. NIGEL MARTYN | 137
6. PEPE REINA | 136
=7. BRAD FRIEDEL | 132
=7. TIM HOWARD | 132
=7. EDWIN VAN DER SAR | 132
10. DAVID DE GEA | 130

UNITED'S INDIVIDUAL STATISTICS

LEAGUE WINNER'S MEDALS

1. RYAN GIGGS | 13
2. PAUL SCHOLES | 11
3. GARY NEVILLE | 8
=4. DENIS IRWIN | 7
=4. ROY KEANE | 7
=6. DAVID BECKHAM | 6
=6. NICKY BUTT | 6
=6. RIO FERDINAND | 6
=6. PHIL NEVILLE | 6
=6. OLE GUNNAR SOLSKJAER | 6

APPEARANCES

1. RYAN GIGGS | 632
2. PAUL SCHOLES | 499
3. GARY NEVILLE | 400
4. WAYNE ROONEY | 393
5. DAVID DE GEA | 377
6. ROY KEANE | 326
7. MICHAEL CARRICK | 316
8. RIO FERDINAND | 312
9. DENIS IRWIN | 296
10. PATRICE EVRA | 273

GOALS

1. WAYNE ROONEY | 183
2. RYAN GIGGS | 109
3. PAUL SCHOLES | 107
4. CRISTIANO RONALDO | 102
5. RUUD VAN NISTELROOY | 95
6. ANDY COLE | 93
7. OLE GUNNAR SOLSKJAER | 91
8. ERIC CANTONA | 64
9. DAVID BECKHAM | 62
10. MARCUS RASHFORD | 59

MARCUS RASHFORD

POSITION ☐ FORWARD

10

"

I'M MY OWN HARSHEST CRITIC AND I KNOW WHEN I'M NOT PLAYING MY BEST FOOTBALL AND I KNOW WHEN I NEED TO IMPROVE. THIS YEAR I HAD TIME TO BREAK, REST, RECOVER MENTALLY AND PHYSICALLY, AND THEN I HAD A PROPER PRE-SEASON. I FEEL REALLY HAPPY.

"

MARCUS ON PROVING
A POINT IN 2022/23

BORN: 31 OCTOBER 1997; MANCHESTER, ENGLAND

After bursting onto the first team scene at Old Trafford in 2016 aged just 18, Marcus Rashford has spent his senior career on fast-forward. The Wythenshawe-born forward racked up appearances quicker than almost any other player in club history, becoming the fourth-youngest Red to pass 200 outings and capturing the imagination with his high-speed approach. Marcus has already experienced the full rollercoaster of fortunes in football, and took a much-needed break at the end of the 2021/22 campaign to recharge his batteries and come back stronger than ever.

"HE'S A BIG THREAT WITH HIS SPEED, HIS ABILITY TO SCORE, HIS DETERMINATION AND HIS FINISHING. HE'S VERY PRECISE, TAKING SHOTS INSIDE AND OUTSIDE OF THE BOX. HE IS SUPER RAPID ON COUNTER-ATTACKS AND IT'S NICE TO SEE GUYS LIKE HIM FROM THE ACADEMY HAVING SUCH A BIG IMPACT IN A BIG, BIG CLUB LIKE UNITED."

CHELSEA MANAGER THOMAS TUCHEL

DID YOU KNOW?

In July 2022, Marcus became guest editor for an edition of famous British comic Beano. In his editor's note, the United and England striker encourages diversity and asks readers to "celebrate all the things that make us unique."

JADON SANCHO

25

DID YOU KNOW?

Jadon has several tattoos on his body, perhaps the most visually striking of which are on his right arm, where he has cartoon tributes to The Simpsons, Sonic the Hedgehog and Spider-Man!

> **I FEEL LIKE EVERYONE HAS SOMETHING TO PROVE. I'M SURE, THIS YEAR, EVERYONE IS GOING TO MAKE UP FOR THAT AND MAKE SURE EVERY GAME WE PLAY WE PUT 100 PER CENT IN AND MAKE SURE THE FANS ARE SMILING AT THE END OF THE GAME.**

JADON ON SMASHING HIS SECOND SEASON AT THE CLUB

Scouted by Watford at just five years old, Jadon Sancho has always been a unique young talent. After his career path took him to Manchester City and Borussia Dortmund, the England trickster joined the Reds ahead of the 2021/22 campaign following a long-term chase from United. While his first campaign didn't pan out precisely how he might have envisaged, Jadon demonstrated his sensational ability and attacking versatility enough times to breed huge optimism that he can be a star of Old Trafford for many years to come.

BORN: 25 MARCH 2000; LONDON, ENGLAND

> "HE'S GROWN IN CONFIDENCE AND GOT USED TO THE UNITED WAY. BRAVER, MORE COURAGE, THOSE LITTLE DETAILS COME FROM CONFIDENCE AND GETTING THAT SWAGGER AND IT'S NICE TO SEE."

FORMER REDS CLUB CAPTAIN ROY KEANE

PREMIER PHOTOGRAPHY

Over three decades of the Premier League, United's club photographers – John Peters, Matt Peters and Ash Donelon – have snapped some iconic moments. We asked the club's long-serving picture desk editor, Simon Davies, to pick out 15 of his favourites and explain his choices…

1993

"Paul Ince and Ryan Giggs wore their favourite jackets for the first ever Premier League trophy celebrations in 1993. Thankfully our kit designers didn't take any notice for the next season's home shirt!"

1993

"Father and son, Peter and Kasper Schmeichel, both Premier League winners - 17 years apart. Trophy parades are always fun, players are always in a good mood which leads to some classic photos."

1994

"Two great captains – Steve Bruce and Bryan Robson – lift the second Premier League trophy in two years. Check out people taking pictures with actual cameras instead of phones!"

2002

"Ruud van Nistelrooy just loved scoring goals – look at the sheer pleasure on his face. And look how sharp the image is, and how blurred the fans are, meaning all your focus is on the main man."

2004

"When a photo captures a player's competitive spirit! Roy Keane never accepted less than 100% from himself or others. You wouldn't want to be on the end of that rant, would you?!"

2007

"It was Gary Neville's dream to score the winner in front of the Kop at Anfield. Unfortunately he didn't do it, but at least John O'Shea did, seconds before this picture was taken – imagine how wild Gary's celebration would have been if he'd actually scored!"

2007

"The first time Nani did this, he caught us all unaware! But thankfully he scored a good few more goals, giving us the chance to capture him in full flight."

2011

"An unbelievable sequence of photos for an amazing goal – it's great in slow-motion but watch it at full speed to see how hard it would be to capture it 'on film'."

2013

"Rio Ferdinand's late goal against Swansea was the last at Old Trafford while Sir Alex Ferguson was Boss, and meant Fergie ended on a high. Not a bad finish for a defender, too!"

2013

"Sir Alex is centre stage, lifting the League trophy after his last home game. And he's just as happy as he was after the first Championship win, 20 years earlier."

2021

"Look at the disappointment on the Brighton players' faces – they know exactly where that ball is going. And what did the two substitutes say to each other? Just a shame there was no crowd…"

2021

"'I've just scored. Where's that photographer? There he is! This way, lads!' Bruno knows how to get on the back pages of all the newspapers – and makes life easy for us!"

2022

"Our photographer used a special filter to make the floodlights look like camera flashbulbs illuminating one of the biggest stars on the planet. An iconic photo of a United icon."

MANCHESTER UNITED WOMEN

MEET THE 2022/23 SQUAD

Captain Katie Zelem introduces each member of the Manchester United Women squad, as Marc Skinner's players continue to grow in both quality and profile...

MARC SKINNER
MANAGER

"Marc has done a great job since he came to the club. I felt like our first season under him was our best season to date. You could see the style he implemented from the off and he was very successful at having us play his way. He's added new signings of his own now, which is important, and he's a really great manager to have at the club. Everyone feels valued and everyone is on the same page."

GOALKEEPERS

27. MARY EARPS

NATIONALITY: ENGLISH
BORN: 7 MARCH 1993

"Mary would have been a fair winner of our Player of the Year award last year. Some of her saves kept us in games at crucial times and it was no surprise to me to see her in such good form at the Euros for England because she just continued her performance levels we see every day."

32. SOPHIE BAGGALEY

NATIONALITY: ENGLISH
BORN: 27 NOVEMBER 1996

"Baggers is our MVP. I've never once heard her moan. Being second-choice goalkeeper is one of the hardest jobs in football but she trains relentlessly, day in, day out. If anyone wants to do extras in training then she's always there and she brings good vibes and energy to the squad every single day."

DEFENDERS

2. ONA BATLLE

NATIONALITY: SPANISH
BORN: 10 JUNE 1999

"Ona came in and won Player of the Year in her first year with the squad, which says everything you need to know about her. She's tenacious, quick, feisty – exactly the type of full-back you want. She's great going forward, loves playing the possession game and is one of our most important players."

3. MARIA THORISDOTTIR

NATIONALITY: NORWEGIAN
BORN: 5 JUNE 1993

"Maria is one of the nicest people in the team. She's got such a warm heart, she's there for anyone who needs anything – she'll always put a smile on people's faces. On the field, she's strong, quick and able to dig us out of a lot of situations defensively."

5. AOIFE MANNION

NATIONALITY: ENGLISH
BORN: 24 SEPTEMBER 1995

"Aoife is everything you would expect in a centre-back: she's strong, quick, physical and someone we missed after she picked up her ACL injury. She's been a huge presence in the dressing room despite her injury, but it'll be a massive boost when she does get back to full fitness."

6. HANNAH BLUNDELL

NATIONALITY: ENGLISH
BORN: 25 MAY 1994

"Like Ona, Hannah has fantastic pace at full-back. She's done so well at left-back considering she's right-footed. She's able to come inside or go down the wing and a lot of our goals have come from the good work she does down the left."

15. MAYA LE TISSIER

NATIONALITY: ENGLISH
BORN: 18 APRIL 2002

"Maya is technically really good, whether she's at centre-back or full-back. Having ball-players across the back four is key for our evolution as a group, and Maya's arrival brings a huge amount of quality to the defence."

DEFENDERS

20. AISSATOU TOUNKARA

NATIONALITY: FRENCH
BORN: 16 MARCH 1995

"I'd never played with Aissa before she joined in the summer, but she arrived with a really good reputation and to be in the France squad at the Euros says all you need to know about her quality. She's going to be a huge addition to the squad and a big presence in defence."

21. MILLIE TURNER

NATIONALITY: ENGLISH
BORN: 7 JULY 1996

"Having Millie back after a spell on the sidelines is like having a new signing. She only played a handful of times last season, but whenever she was involved the team just looked so solid. She's a huge character on and off the pitch, and her leadership brings everyone forward with her."

MIDFIELDERS

4. JADE MOORE

NATIONALITY: ENGLISH
BORN: 22 OCTOBER 1990

" Jade came midway through the 2021/22 season and quickly showed that she was a great addition. She brought a lot of experience for club and country, she's played under Marc before so she knows his style and she likes to guide the people around her."

8. VILDE BOE RISA

NATIONALITY: NORWEGIAN
BORN: 13 JULY 1995

"Vilde is technically unbelievable. Her one-touch, two-touch play is sensational and she can always pick a pass. The detail in her game is phenomenal. She's very direct in how she speaks, but she does it in a really nice way!"

10. KATIE ZELEM

NATIONALITY: ENGLISH
BORN: 20 JANUARY 1996

"I'm just so proud to be Manchester United captain. It's a lot of responsibility but it's a massive honour. I've got a great relationship with Marc and that makes the role so much more enjoyable – we can be open and honest with each other, and he was a big reason in me extending my contract."

12. HAYLEY LADD

NATIONALITY: WELSH
BORN: 6 OCTOBER 1993

"We like to call Hayley 'Octopus Legs' because nobody can get past her. Whenever we do one-v-one defending, she's the one person you don't want to be against. That side of her game is fantastic and so valuable for the squad. She's also the most chilled person you'll ever meet!"

14. JACKIE GROENEN

NATIONALITY: DUTCH
BORN: 17 DECEMBER 1994

"Jackie's unbelievable at pressing. Her energy and intensity all over the pitch, how she hassles for the ball and wins it back for us, is priceless. It's key to have someone like that in your team. A lot goes on in the game that doesn't involve goals, and Jackie is massive for us in that sense."

26. GRACE CLINTON

NATIONALITY: ENGLISH
BORN: 31 MARCH 2003

"Grace is honestly going to be a phenomenal player. I sometimes forget how young she is because some of the things she does in training and in games is sensational. She's a great fit for United and there's so much more still to come from her."

37. LUCY STANIFORTH

NATIONALITY: ENGLISH
BORN: 2 OCTOBER 1992

"Like Vilde, Lucy is technically brilliant. She hits a ball like I've never seen. She could hit a ball now and it would still be travelling next week! She can play in different positions and brings a different type of threat wherever she operates. Lucy guarantees a big contribution."

FORWARDS

7. ELLA TOONE

NATIONALITY: ENGLISH
BORN: 2 SEPTEMBER 1999

"Tooney had a great impact at the Euros, which was just an extension of the brilliant work she did for us during 2021/22. She's got so much talent and she provides so many goals and assists that she's just a really important player for us."

9. MARTHA THOMAS

NATIONALITY: SCOTTISH
BORN: 31 MAY 1996

"Thommo is lightning quick with unbelievable movement. Last year she spent a lot of time on the right wing, a new position for her, but she made it her own and really grew into it. By the end of the season, you'd have thought she'd been a right winger all her career, her crosses were that good."

11. LEAH GALTON

NATIONALITY: ENGLISH
BORN: 24 MAY 1994

"When Leah's on her game, she's one of the best forwards you'll come across. Her pace, strength, power, left foot… the list is endless and she's definitely someone you want on your team rather than against you!"

17. LUCIA GARCIA

NATIONALITY: SPANISH
BORN: 14 JULY 1998

"Lucia is so fast and she can play off the left, the right or down the middle and we really need that versatility. We've got a lot of forwards but it's key for us to have that interchangeability. Lucia quickly showed her quality in training after she signed, and I think she'll be a great addition."

18. KIRSTY HANSON

NATIONALITY: SCOTTISH
BORN: 17 APRIL 1998

"Lightning fast, super powerful – if there's someone you don't want running at you in training, it's Kirky! Her pace and change of direction are second to none. One of only two left-footers in the team, so she's really valuable for us."

19. ADRIANA LEON

NATIONALITY: CANADA
BORN: 2 OCTOBER 1992

"Marc has done a great job bringing pace into our attack and the signing of Dri is a big part of that. She's got great pedigree, having won Olympic gold with Canada, and a vast amount of experience, plus she can play multiple positions so I see her being a great addition."

22. NIKITA PARRIS

NATIONALITY: ENGLISH
BORN: 10 MARCH 1994

"Keets is a really good friend of mine and I think she'll be a huge signing on and off the pitch. She's my new locker buddy and I'm excited to have her here. I think this is her year to come back into her own and she's shown at some of her previous clubs just how devastating an attacker she can be."

23. ALESSIA RUSSO

NATIONALITY: ENGLISH
BORN: 8 FEBRUARY 1999

"Our Player of the Year last year, as voted for by the players, which is one of the biggest honours you can have. Lessi scored really important goals for us, game-changing goals, and she deserves all the success she's had at club and international level, where she has been fantastic for England."

28. RACHEL WILLIAMS

NATIONALITY: ENGLISH
BORN: 10 JANUARY 1988

"Rachel is a great character to have around the club. She has a lot of experience, brings great maturity to the squad and that's vital when you're striving to keep improving as a group. She guides younger players and is a really good addition in that respect."

PUSHING THE GAME FORWARD

On the back of England's sensational campaign at Euro 2022, Katie looks forward to women's football going from strength to strength…

"Euro 2022 was a really exciting time for football in general, not just women's football. It was a huge event and so many people got behind it. A lot of players and prominent figures in the men's game were getting in touch to send love and support to the England team, which is fantastic. I sat next to Declan Rice at the final at Wembley, which just went to show how the whole country was behind the team. Personally, it was fantastic to see not only my team-mates win, but also people who have been my friends for years. Mary was unbelievable, getting the most clean sheets in the tournament and making key saves early on in matches to keep England in games, Alessia scored the most goals as a substitute in any Euros tournament and Ella made a massive contribution too – not just by scoring in the final. All three of them were fantastic across the whole tournament.

"The viewing figures on television were phenomenal and one of the best aspects was the size of the attendances at games throughout the tournament. Obviously, England had some massive numbers turning up – almost 90,000 at the final – but there were games which didn't involve the host nation that were reaching 25,000, and that shows how many travelling fans there were and how high interest was across the board. It was great to see so many people out supporting the Euros at Old Trafford as well, so it'll be brilliant to be playing there with United Women in 2022/23. It was a dream for me to score when we beat Everton at OT in 2021/22 and I'd love to do the same again, but the main thing is that attendances continue to increase wherever we play, whether it's at Old Trafford, Leigh Sports Village or any of our away games. For me and everyone involved in women's football, it would be amazing to see the hype and attraction of the Euros continue and directed towards the WSL. We want to harness that legacy and keep pushing the women's game forward."

- KATIE ZELEM, AUGUST 2022

CHAMPIONS

THE LIONESSES

MARY
EARPS

ELLA
TOONE

ALESSIA
RUSSO

THE KIDS WON THE CUP!

United regained the prestigious FA Youth Cup for a record 11th time in 2021/22. Here's how the Reds returned to the summit of youth football, and why no other club can match our record…

"I'M SO PROUD OF THIS FOOTBALL CLUB AND THE ACADEMY. IT'S A REMARKABLE CLUB TO BE INVOLVED WITH AND I THINK WE NEED TO REMIND OURSELVES OF THAT AT TIMES."

Under-18s lead coach Travis Binnion was left almost speechless as United lifted the FA Youth Cup in May 2022, courtesy of a hard-fought 3-1 win over Nottingham Forest at Old Trafford.

The triumph marked a full-circle journey for the young Reds, whose road to the final began in M16 with a third round win over Scunthorpe United, who were beaten 4-2. United hit the road in round four, winning 3-1 at Reading, before returning to the Theatre of Dreams to defeat Everton (4-1), Leicester City (2-1) and Wolverhampton Wanderers (3-0). Forest's visit prompted an all-time competition record attendance of 67,492, and those inside Old Trafford were treated to a happy ending after a close encounter.

Skipper Rhys Bennett headed in the first-half opener for Binnion's Reds, only for Josh Powell to draw the visitors level on the stroke of half-time. Just as extra-time loomed, however, Argentina forward Alejandro Garnacho won and scored a penalty, then added a late third – his seventh in the competition – to wrap up a memorable night for United's latest crop of FA Youth Cup winners.

As Binnion put it in his post-match interview: "I knew this football club was special, but I've been blown away tonight!"

THE PERFECT SUPPORT

After a record attendance crammed into Old Trafford to witness the Reds' win over Nottingham Forest, Nick Cox – head of the club's Academy – thanked the United fanbase in an open letter…

"As head of Academy, I have a duty to support the development of young players and in doing so ensure that we create amazing experiences that enrich their lives. It is fair to say that the record attendance, passion and atmosphere inside Old Trafford will stay with this group forever and stand every single one of our players in great stead for the remainder of their careers. It was a truly magical night which reminded everyone of the importance of youth to the culture of Manchester and this great football club. For some of our players, it will be the first of many times that they will have the privilege of playing in front of a packed and roaring Old Trafford crowd. For others, it may well be the height of their careers and possibly the best night of their lives. We consider the Academy to be family, one that people never leave regardless of where they go in life. The same can certainly be said of the United fanbase. The Academy and our loyal supporters remain the lifeblood of Manchester United."

- NICK COX, HEAD OF ACADEMY

UNITED'S YOUTH CUP FINAL WINS

Here are the aggregate scores from all of the Reds' FAYC final triumphs:

1952/53	**UNITED 9**	WOLVES 3	
1953/54	**UNITED 5**	WOLVES 4	
1954/55	**UNITED 7**	WEST BROM 1	
1955/56	**UNITED 4**	CHESTERFIELD 3	
1956/57	**UNITED 8**	WEST HAM 2	
1963/64	**UNITED 5**	SWINDON TOWN 2	
1991/92	**UNITED 6**	CRYSTAL PALACE 3	
1994/95	**UNITED 2**	SPURS 2 (4-3 ON PENALTIES)	
2002/03	**UNITED 3**	MIDDLESBROUGH 1	
2010/11	**UNITED 6**	SHEFFIELD UNITED 3	
2021/22	**UNITED 3**	NOTTINGHAM FOREST 1*	

*one-legged format

MOST FA YOUTH CUP TROPHIES

1. MANCHESTER UNITED - 11

2. CHELSEA - 9

3. ARSENAL - 7

=4. ASTON VILLA - 4

=4. LIVERPOOL - 4

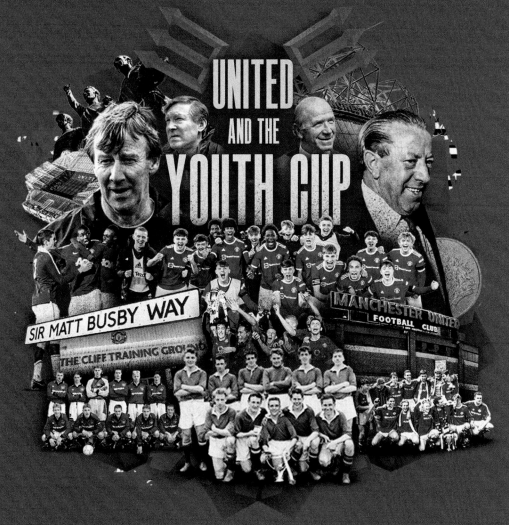

UNITED AND THE YOUTH CUP

SIR MATT BUSBY WAY

THE CLIFF TRAINING GROUND

MANCHESTER UNITED FOOTBALL CLUB

WORDSEARCH

Can you locate the surnames of the Reds' top 10 appearance-makers in the Premier League?

E	K	D	N	A	N	I	D	R	E	F
G	E	E	U	S	G	I	G	G	S	O
Z	P	Q	A	R	E	A	W	S	A	Z
I	R	I	O	N	D	L	U	R	M	J
E	L	L	I	V	E	N	O	M	I	R
Y	F	I	B	C	O	A	A	H	I	Q
E	E	F	H	D	E	G	E	A	C	A
R	O	O	N	E	Y	Q	A	K	R	S
D	A	D	X	I	R	Y	W	V	W	Z
C	A	R	R	I	C	K	E	C	M	S

GIGGS	SCHOLES	NEVILLE	ROONEY	DE GEA
KEANE	CARRICK	FERDINAND	IRWIN	EVRA

LANDMARK GOALS

Can you match these landmark Premier League goals to the scorers?

FIRST PREMIER LEAGUE GOAL

FIRST PREMIER LEAGUE GOAL AT OLD TRAFFORD

FIRST PREMIER LEAGUE MATCHWINNING GOAL

1999 TITLE CLINCHER

HALFWAY LINE GOAL

UNITED'S 1,000TH PREMIER LEAGUE GOAL

GOAL ON 500TH UNITED APPEARANCE

GOAL ON CLUB RECORD 758TH UNITED APPEARANCE

19TH LEAGUE TITLE CLINCHER

UNITED'S 2,000TH PL GOAL

DION DUBLIN
V SOUTHAMPTON

WAYNE ROONEY
V BLACKBURN

SCOTT McTOMINAY
V NORWICH

MARK HUGHES
V SHEFFIELD UNITED

PAUL SCHOLES
V LIVERPOOL

ANDY COLE
V TOTTENHAM

RYAN GIGGS
V WIGAN

CRISTIANO RONALDO
V MIDDLESBROUGH

DENIS IRWIN
V IPSWICH

DAVID BECKHAM
V WIMBLEDON

ANSWERS ON PAGE 60

GOAL OR NO GOAL?

Take a look at some of these action shots from United's Premier League back catalogue. Of the 10 pictures, can you tell which five resulted in goals and which five didn't?

ROONEY V NEWCASTLE

KEANE V BIRMINGHAM

TEVEZ V PORTSMOUTH

RONALDO V WIGAN

BERBATOV V CITY

WELBECK V LIVERPOOL

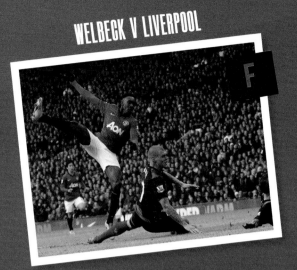

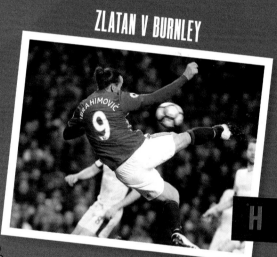

DI MARIA V LEICESTER

ZLATAN V BURNLEY

LUKAKU V STOKE

BRUNO V VILLA

AWAY DAYS

Yes or no – have United played at least one away game in the Premier League at these ten grounds?

1. VILLA PARK

2. WEMBLEY STADIUM

3. DEEPDALE

4. STAMFORD BRIDGE

5. ASHTON GATE

6. EWOOD PARK

7. STADIUM MK

8. THE DEN

9. TURF MOOR

10. MEADOW LANE

SCORING DEBUT ANAGRAMS

Below are five jumbled-up names of players who scored on their Premier League debut for United – can you unscramble their names using the hints?

1. LONE JAGUAR SNORKELS _____
(Hint: Norwegian striker who fired home against Blackburn in 1996)

2. HAILING BREEZE _____
(Hint: Argentinian defender who volleyed in at Bolton in 2004)

3. MANY A TRIATHLON _____
(Hint: French striker who made an instant impact against Liverpool in 2015)

4. JAILED NAMES _____
(Hint: Welsh winger who wrapped up a big opening day win over Chelsea in 2019)

5. BEAN DONKEY VEND _____
(Hint: Dutch midfielder who slotted home against Crystal Palace in 2020)

ANSWERS ON PAGE 61

STEPPING UP

When a player leaves United, their vacant shirt number is invariably filled by a new player. Can you recall who replaced each of the following legends?

A

Edwin van der Sar's no.1 shirt was taken by...

B

David Beckham's no.7 shirt was taken by...

C

Gary Neville's no.2 shirt was taken by...

D

Louis Saha's no.9 shirt was taken by...

E

Rio Ferdinand's no.5 shirt was taken by...

F

Paul Scholes's no.18 shirt was taken by...

G

Juan Mata's no.8 shirt was taken by...

H

Roy Keane's no.16 shirt was taken by...

I

Nani's no.17 shirt was taken by...

ANSWERS ON PAGE 61

PREMIER LEAGUE DEBUTS

Can you match the player to the opposition team they made their PL debut against?

 JUAN MATA

 NICKY BUTT

 CRISTIANO RONALDO

 JADON SANCHO

 PATRICE EVRA

 RAPHAEL VARANE

 JAMES GARNER

 ANDY COLE

 SCOTT McTOMINAY

 ROBIN VAN PERSIE

 ALEJANDRO GARNACHO

 KIKO MACHEDA

 DIMITAR BERBATOV

 JUAN SEBASTIAN VERON

 QUINTON FORTUNE

CHELSEA (2021/22)

WOLVES (2021/22)

LEEDS UNITED (2021/22)

CRYSTAL PALACE (2018/19)

ARSENAL (2016/17)

CARDIFF CITY (2013/14)

EVERTON (2012/13)

ASTON VILLA (2008/09)

LIVERPOOL (2008/09)

MANCHESTER CITY (2005/06)

BOLTON WANDERERS (2003/04)

FULHAM (2001/02)

NEWCASTLE (1999/2000)

BLACKBURN ROVERS (1994/95)

OLDHAM ATHLETIC (1992/93)

WHOSE ASSIST?

United have netted some famously brilliant Premier League goals down the years – but can you remember which players provided the assist for each of these 10?

If you need help with this quiz, why not watch the goals on YouTube to identify the assist-makers!

1996/97
ERIC CANTONA'S CHIP V SUNDERLAND

1998/99
ANDY COLE'S TITLE-WINNING LOB V TOTTENHAM

1999/2000
PAUL SCHOLES'S VOLLEY FROM A CORNER AT BRADFORD CITY

2010/11
WAYNE ROONEY'S OVERHEAD KICK V MANCHESTER CITY

2012/13
ROBIN VAN PERSIE'S VOLLEY AGAINST ASTON VILLA

2014/15
JUAN MATA'S SCISSOR KICK V LIVERPOOL AT ANFIELD

2015/16
ANTHONY MARTIAL'S DEBUT GOAL V LIVERPOOL

2016/17
HENRIKH MKHITARYAN'S SCORPION KICK AGAINST SUNDERLAND

2020/21
BRUNO FERNANDES'S LOBBED SHOT V EVERTON AT OLD TRAFFORD

2021/22
CRISTIANO RONALDO'S LONG-RANGE SHOT AGAINST TOTTENHAM

ANSWERS ON PAGE 61

LANDMARK GOALS

First Premier League goal | Mark Hughes v Sheffield United

First Premier League goal at Old Trafford | Denis Irwin v Ipswich

First Premier League matchwinning goal | Dion Dublin v Southampton

1999 title clincher | Andy Cole v Tottenham

Halfway line goal | David Beckham v Wimbledon

United's 1,000th Premier League goal | Cristiano Ronaldo v Middlesbrough

Goal on 500th United appearance | Paul Scholes v Liverpool

Goal on club record 758th United appearance | Ryan Giggs v Wigan

19th league title clincher | Wayne Rooney v Blackburn

United's 2,000th PL goal | Scott McTominay v Norwich

WORDSEARCH

```
E  K  D  N  A  N  I  D  R  E  F
G  E  E  U  S  G  I  G  G  S  O
Z  P  Q  A  R  E  A  W  S  A  Z
I  R  I  O  N  D  L  U  R  M  J
E  L  L  I  V  E  N  O  M  I  R
Y  F  I  B  C  O  A  A  H  I  Q
E  E  F  H  D  E  G  E  A  C  A
R  O  O  N  E  Y  Q  A  K  R  S
D  A  D  X  I  R  Y  W  V  W  Z
C  A  R  R  I  C  K  E  C  M  S
```

GOAL OR NO GOAL?

A. Keane v Birmingham – GOAL
B. Rooney v Newcastle – GOAL
C. Tevez v Portsmouth – NO GOAL
D. Ronaldo v Wigan – GOAL
E. Berbatov v City – NO GOAL
F. Welbeck v Liverpool – NO GOAL
G. Di Maria v Leicester – GOAL
H. Zlatan v Burnley – NO GOAL
I. Lukaku v Stoke – GOAL
J. Bruno v Villa – NO GOAL

AWAY DAYS

1. Villa Park – YES
2. Wembley Stadium – YES
3. Deepdale – NO
4. Stamford Bridge – YES
5. Ashton Gate – NO
6. Ewood Park – YES
7. Stadium MK – NO
8. The Den – NO
9. Turf Moor – YES
10. Meadow Lane – NO

SCORING DEBUT ANAGRAMS

1. Ole Gunnar Solskjaer
2. Gabriel Heinze
3. Anthony Martial
4. Daniel James
5. Donny van de Beek

STEPPING UP

A. David De Gea
B. Cristiano Ronaldo
C. Rafael da Silva
D. Dimitar Berbatov
E. Marcos Rojo
F. Ashley Young
G. Bruno Fernandes
H. Michael Carrick
I. Daley Blind

PREMIER LEAGUE DEBUTS

Alejandro Garnacho – Chelsea (2021/22)
Raphael Varane – Wolves (2021/22)
Jadon Sancho – Leeds United (2021/22)
James Garner – Crystal Palace (2018/19)
Scott McTominay – Arsenal (2016/17)
Juan Mata – Cardiff City (2013/14)
Robin van Persie – Everton (2012/13)
Kiko Macheda – Aston Villa (2008/09)
Dimitar Berbatov – Liverpool (2008/09)
Patrice Evra – Manchester City (2005/06)
Cristiano Ronaldo – Bolton Wanderers (2003/04)
Juan Sebastian Veron – Fulham (2001/02)
Quinton Fortune – Newcastle (1999/2000)
Andy Cole – Blackburn Rovers (1994/95)
Nicky Butt – Oldham Athletic (1992/93)

WHOSE ASSIST?

1. Brian McClair
2. Gary Neville
3. David Beckham
4. Nani
5. Wayne Rooney
6. Angel Di Maria
7. Ashley Young
8. Zlatan Ibrahimovic
9. Aaron Wan-Bissaka
10. Fred

COMPETITION TIME!

ONE LUCKY READER IS GOING TO WIN A 2022/23 UNITED SHIRT SIGNED BY FIRST TEAM MEMBERS.

TO STAND A CHANCE OF WINNING, SIMPLY ANSWER THIS REMARKABLY EASY QUESTION:

WHICH PLAYER TOOK UNITED'S NO.8 SHIRT AFTER JUAN MATA'S DEPARTURE IN THE SUMMER OF 2022?

A. DAVID DE GEA

B. BRUNO FERNANDES

C. DIOGO DALOT

TO ENTER, JUST VISIT
MANUTD.COM/ANNUAL2023

GOOD LUCK!